Music from the Days
of
GEORGE WASHINGTON

A COLLECTION OF
PATRIOTIC AND MILITARY TUNES
PIANO AND DANCE MUSIC
SONGS AND OPERATIC AIRS

———

UNITED STATES
GEORGE WASHINGTON BICENTENNIAL COMMISSION
Washington, D. C.

Music from the Days of George Washington

COLLECTED AND PROVIDED WITH
AN INTRODUCTION BY

CARL ENGEL
Chief, Division of Music,
Library of Congress

———

THE MUSIC EDITED BY

W. OLIVER STRUNK
Assistant, Division of Music,
Library of Congress

———

WITH A PREFACE BY

HON. SOL BLOOM
Associate Director
United States George Washington Bicentennial Commission

✿

AMS PRESS
NEW YORK

Reprinted from the edition of 1931, Washington, D.C.
First AMS EDITION published 1970
Manufactured in the United States of America

International Standard Book Number: 0-404-07230-5
Library of Congress Number: 73-136418

AMS PRESS INC.
NEW YORK, N.Y. 10003

PREFACE

THE United States George Washington Bicentennial Commission is issuing this selection of eighteenth century music as an important contribution to the general program for observing the Two-Hundredth Anniversary of the Birth of George Washington, in 1932.

It is proper in the formation of a general program for the celebration that music should be given a conspicuous place in the detail of ceremonies and observances. A great amount of music suitable for the purpose is available, in a variety of forms, including some that has been especially written for the occasion. But music dating from the days of George Washington himself is rare and can be found only in libraries and historical collections.

This Commission, therefore, has considered it helpful and appropriate to issue, for distribution, this collection of eighteenth century music intimately connected with the historic period of our national origin.

The sincere and strong character of this music accords well with the rugged simplicity from which sprang the faith and vision that laid the foundation of our Republic.

SOL BLOOM
Associate Director
United States George Washington
Bicentennial Commission

SEPTEMBER 29, 1931

INTRODUCTION

IT required the solemn celebration of the two-hundredth anniversary of George Washington's birth to prepare this volume of music. The collection could, and properly should, have been compiled before this. If it does not reveal musical treasures hitherto unknown or of great price, it clearly reflects a whole epoch—of foremost importance in the history of our nation—an epoch which loudly resounded with the tumult of war, but not to the exclusion of more peaceful strains. Fife and drum did not silence harpsichord and flute. And while the occasion has governed the choice, the music represented here is not entirely of an "occasional" character, seeking apologetic shelter under merely "historical associations."

Such associations, of course, exist in the majority of cases. As befits the purpose, they are directly or indirectly connected with George Washington. The soldier has been ranked with Frederick the Great and the first Napoleon. Of the illustrious trio, only the Prussian King had decided musical tastes and talents. But both Napoleon and Washington valued music as an indispensable adjunct to military, social, and religious functions; and neither of the two was spared the numerous and varied musical tributes paid to his person and glory, in accordance with the fashion of the times.

When Dr. Charles Burney, the English historian of music, visited Prague, capital of Bohemia, in 1772, he wrote: "A great part of the town is new, as scarce a single building escaped the Prussian batteries and bombardment during the blockade, in the last war." Frederick's military feat moved an otherwise unremembered composer to write a piece for the piano entitled "The Battle of Prague," enormously popular among the least bellicose of musical amateurs far into the first half of the nineteenth century. Napoleon's spectacular victory at Marengo was similarly illustrated in tones, and many editions of this battle-piece were published, not only in Europe but in the young United States. True to form, an American composer, James Hewitt, was inspired by Washington's signal achievement at the battle of Trenton to write an elaborate "historical military Sonata," first printed anonymously in 1797.

As the late O. G. Sonneck has pointed out in a study of "The Musical Side of Our First Presidents," George Washington, man of the world that he was, did not shrink from attending concerts, dances, or performances of the then prevailing English ballad-operas. Personal modesty, however, may have made these musical events a little irksome, whenever they turned into personal ovations. At least there is a curious account in the German periodical, "Magazin der Musik" (Vol. II, 1784), edited by Carl Friedrich Cramer, telling of a concert given in Philadelphia in 1783, which was attended by General Washington. The concert was to have ended with the singing of an "Ode" written in his honor. When he learned of this, he is said to have taken leave before the concert was over. We are therefore left to wonder what were Washington's real feelings when, on April 21, 1789—on his journey to New York for his inauguration as first President—he was greeted at Trenton[1] by "a white-robed choir who met him with the congratulatory song"[2] before a triumphal arch erected on the bridge that spanned the Assanpink Creek. Washington handsomely thanked "the matrons and young ladies" for their musical offering. On this occasion the narrow bridge left no other means of progress or egress.

It is certain that Washington liked good company; and company of any sort, in his day, meant musical accompaniment. If it were argued that such public attendance, in an official capacity, did not necessarily prove Washington to have been a lover of music, there would remain the fact that apparently he listened with enjoyment to the playing and singing of his adopted daughter, Nelly Custis, in the family circle at Mount Vernon. Arnold's "The Wayworn Traveller," tradition says, was one of the songs with which she delighted him most often during the last quiet months of his own eventful journey.

[1]See "The New Jersey Journal and Political Intelligencer," Elizabeth, N. J., May 6, 1789; cf. also Dr. C. E. Godfrey's article in "Trenton Sunday Advertiser," Dec. 29, 1912, pages 19 and 20.

[2]The words by Major Richard Howell, adapted for the occasion to Handel's chorus "See, the conqu'ring hero comes," and later published with music specially composed by Alexander Reinagle.

Washington attended Christ (Episcopal) Church in Alexandria. It is not likely, however, that he joined in the hymns. He avowed himself incapable of raising a note; and he probably was too considerate of the proprieties—if not too musical—to add one more discordant voice to a choir which probably suffered no lack of them.

Practical considerations have limited the selection of music offered in this volume. Nevertheless, it may claim to present a fairly complete cross-section of the secular music that was heard in America during the latter half of Washington's life. Purely political songs (such as "The Battle of the Kegs," sung to the tune of "Yankee Doodle," or "Adams and Liberty," adapted to the convivial air of "Anacreon in Heaven" composed by the Englishman John Stafford Smith, long before Francis Scott Key wedded to it his poem known as "The Star-Spangled Banner") have been purposely excluded. So has religious or church music, of which there existed almost as many different kinds as there were denominations or sects in a country that gave freedom of worship to all of them. Some of these church hymns (as, for instance, the fine tune "Coronation" by Oliver Holden [1765-1844] of Charlestown, Mass., which is still sung to the hymn beginning "All hail the pow'r of Jesus' name!") are still in use, or have been especially collected and are easily available.[1] Of both a religious and patriotic character was the hymn known as "Chester,"[1] the words and music of which were written about 1778 by William Billings [1746-1800], tanner and "singing-master." It was a great favorite among the Continental troops in the North and South. The thirst for freedom in some of these revolutionary composers extended to strange liberties which they took with the laws of musical harmony as then established.

*   *

*

A few words of comment on the music contained in this volume may be helpful. The first part comprises samples of patriotic and military music. They date from the Revolutionary and post-Revolutionary periods. "The President's

March" was probably composed by Philip Phile, a German music-teacher, who settled in Philadelphia after 1771. The earliest known edition of this march was published about 1793; which does not mean that it may not have been composed and in use before that year, since most of this military music was copied and re-copied by hand, as is shown by numerous manuscript tune-books of the time that have come down to us, in many of which this march is recorded, thus proving its immediate and wide-spread popularity. Upon this popularity was conferred a degree of permanence when, in 1798, Joseph Hopkinson wrote for it his poem "Hail, Columbia!", which has become one of our most stirring national airs.

The next number, "Washington's March," was also called "Washington's Grand March" and "The New President's March." It is not impossible that this is the oldest among the several variants of Washington marches, since references to it have been found in American newspapers as early as 1784. But its seniority is not absolutely established. Nor has there been brought to light, so far, any convincing proof that this march was written by Francis Hopkinson [1737-1791], the first native-born American composer and one of the signers of the Declaration of Independence, a man of such manifold gifts and signal accomplishments that it seems only natural to see in him the author of something which he certainly had the skill and ability to write. There is no doubt, however, concerning Hopkinson's authorship of the words and music of "The Toast." The poem was printed in the "Pennsylvania Packet" on April 8, 1778. Apparently the earliest and only printed issue of the music and words was not brought out until 21 years later, when Benjamin Carr, the Philadelphia publisher, advertised it in the Philadelphia newspapers, in March, 1799. It was issued jointly with "Brother soldiers, all hail! A favorite new patriotic song in honor of Washington," the words of which were adapted to "Washington's March." There will be another reference to Hopkinson later.[2]

[1]See "Ye olde New England psalm-tunes, 1620-1820, with historical sketch by William Arms Fisher, Boston, Oliver Ditson Co., 1930; cf. also "American writers and compilers of sacred music," by Frank J. Metcalf, The Abingdon Press, New York and Cincinnati, 1925.

[2]A copy of this extremely rare publication is in the music collection of the Boston Public Library.

A manuscript copy of the words and music of "The Toast" marked "composed by F. H. Esq.," once part of the library of Michael Hillegas [1729-1804], the first Treasurer of the United States, was accidentally found in 1931 by Mr. Edward Hopkinson, a descendant of Francis, in the Philadelphia shop of Henry C. Woehlcke, where Mr. John Tasker Howard kindly copied it for use in this collection.

"General Burgoyne's March" is taken from a manuscript band book in the Library of Congress, inscribed "The property of the Bellamy Band, June 1799," the Bellamy in question being probably Col. Samuel Bellamy of Hamden, Conn. The name of a British General as title of the march is indication of its origin. It also shows that the American army bands had evidently no scruples about appropriating a good tune, even if it happened to be the enemy's. The same applies to the "Brandywine Quick-Step" (the engagement that gave the march its name was fought between General Howe and Washington on Sept. 11, 1777), which remained popular with American bands for some years, since it was still included in Blake's "The Martial Music of Camp Dupont," a collection of military tunes published in Philadelphia after 1815.

"Successful Campaign" appears in Thompson's, the London publisher's, "Twenty-Four Country Dances for the Year 1769" with the title "Successfull Campain; or, Bath Frollick." The Bath referred to, was, of course, the fashionable English spa. In connection with this tune, Dr. John C. Fitzpatrick, the editor of Washington's papers and eminent authority on all matters pertaining to his life, has recorded the following characteristic incident:

"When the French army arrived at Rhode Island, the Continental drums were thrown somewhat in the background by the more showy bands of Rochambeau's force. On Washington's visit to Newport in March 1781, to confer with the French commander, the French officers arranged a ball in his honor. They decorated the ballroom with flags, swords, drums, streamers and all the fanciful color that the army possessed, and George Washington opened the ball by request. He danced the first number with Miss Margaret Champlin, one of the reigning belles of Newport, and, as the signal was given, the French officers took the instruments from the hands of their musicians and flourished the opening strains of "A Successful Campaign," which piece Miss Champlin had chosen as the one with which the ball should open.

"It proved a prophetic choice for, eight months afterwards, the two generals present at that Newport ball finished a successful campaign by forcing the surrender of Cornwallis at Yorktown. . . ."[1]

Reference has already been made to Hewitt's Sonata, entitled "The Battle of Trenton" and dedicated to Washington. It is neither better nor worse than a great many similar descriptive pieces of the period, by means of which the player

[1] John C. Fitzpatrick, "The Bands of the Continental Army," in his *Spirit of the Revolution*, p. 173.

sought to procure for the delicate sensibilities of the tender sex, assembled in the drawing-room, the thrill and emotions attendant upon the bloody clash of arms. The "Washington's March" introduced in this Sonata is usually called "Washington's March at the Battle of Trenton" (found also under the titles of "The President's New March" and "General Wayne's March"). This military Sonata crosses the border-line into the second group of pieces, which comprises samples of the kind of music that Washington and his contemporaries heard at concerts and social gatherings.

* *
*

In Washington's diaries and account books there are numerous entries which permit a fair idea of what sort of musical affairs he was apt to attend. One such concert in particular—given by Alexander Reinagle in Philadelphia, on June 12, 1787—is notable for its program, which follows:

ACT I.

Overture	[John Christian] Bach
Concerto Violoncello	Capron
Song	Sarti

ACT II.

Overture	André
Concerto Violin	Fiorillo
Concerto Flute	Brown

ACT III.

Overture (La Buona Figliuola)	Piccini
Sonata Pianoforte	Reinagle
A New Overture (in which is introduced a Scotch Strathspey)	Reinagle

Alexander Reinagle (of Portsmouth and London), William Brown (*recte* Wilhelm Braun, of Cassel, and probably a former member of a Hessian Band!), and Henri Capron (of Paris?), the three composer-performers who appeared as soloists, contributed much to musical life in America during the last years of the eighteenth century. On the concert programs of Washington's time composers' and performers' names were often indiscriminately interchanged; it is therefore impossible to say with certainty whether Reinagle and his friends played original compositions. But it is more than likely that the "Sonata Pianoforte" that figures on this program was one of four such works, which, in the composers's handwriting, are now in the Library of Congress. The first movement of one of these Reinagle Sonatas, not hitherto published, is here included. The manuscript is not dated, but the notation "Philadelphia" indicates that it was written after 1786, the year of Reinagle's arrival in this country. Brown is represented by the first of his "Three Rondos for the Piano Forte or Harpsichord" (1787), dedicated to Francis Hopkinson.

From a Library of Congress manuscript in the autograph of Pierre Landrin Duport (a French dancing-master who fled from Paris after the storming of the Bastille, July 14, 1789, and emigrated to the United States) are taken the four dances that complete the second group of pieces. Their titles, as written by Duport himself, are "Minuetto & Gavott, Compos'd by Alxr. Reinagle Esqr.," "Fancy Menuit Dance before Genl. Washington 1792," and "Fancy Menuit with figure Dance by Two young Ladies in the presance of Mrs. Washington in 1792. Phila." Let us trust that the gentleman's choreography was better than his orthography.

The first place among the vocal pieces chosen has naturally been accorded to one of the most attractive of the eight songs that Francis Hopkinson, in 1788, dedicated to Washington as a mark of his affection and esteem. "This little Work . . . is such as a Lover, not a Master, of the Arts can furnish," Hopkinson writes in his letter of dedication. "I am neither a profess'd Poet, nor a profess'd Musician; and yet venture to appear in those characters united; for which, I confess, the censure of Temerity may justly be brought against me. . . . However small the Reputation may be that I shall derive from this Work, I cannot, I believe, be refused the Credit of being the first Native of the United States who has produced a Musical Composition. If this attempt should not be too severely treated, others may be encouraged to venture on a path, yet untrodden in America, and the Arts in succession will take root and flourish amongst us." Washington's gracious letter of acceptance is too characteristic not to merit another reprint in full:

Mount Vernon Feby 5th, 1789.

Dear Sir,

We are told of the amazing powers of Musick in ancient times; but the stories of its effects are so surprising that we are not obliged to believe them, unless they had been founded upon better authority than Poetic assertion—for the Poets of old (whatever they may do in these days) were strangely addicted to the marvellous,—and if I before *doubted* the truth of their relations with respect to the power of Musick, I am now fully convinced of their falsity—because I would not, for the honor of my Country, allow that we are left by the ancients at an *immeasurable* distance in everything,—and if they could sooth the ferocity of wild beasts—could draw the trees & the stones after them—and could even charm the powers of Hell by their Musick, I am sure that your productions would have had at least virtue enough in them (without the aid of voice or instrument) to soften the Ice of the Delaware & Potomack—and in that case you should have had an earlier acknowledgment of your favor of the 1st of December which came to hand but last Saturday.—

I readily admit the force of your distinction between "a thing *done*" and "a thing *to be done*"—and as I do not believe that you would do "a very bad thing indeed" I must even make a virtue of necessity, and defend your performance, if necessary, to the last effort of my musical abilities.—

But, my dear Sir, if you had any doubts about the reception which your work would meet with—or had the smallest reason to think that you should need any assistance to defend it—you have not acted with your usual good judgment in the choice of a Coadjutor;—for, should the tide of prejudice not flow in favor of it (and so various are the tastes, opinions & whims of men, that even the sanction of Divinity does not ensure universal concurrence) what, alas! can I do to support it?—I can neither sing one of the songs, nor raise a single note on any instrument to convince the unbelieving.—But I have, however, one argument which will prevail with persons of true taste (at least in America)—I can tell them that *it is the production of Mr. Hopkinson.*

With the compliments of Mrs. Washington added to mine, for you & yours

I am—Dear Sir
Your most Obedt and
very Hble Servant
Go. Washington.

Hopkinson's song is followed by "Delia, a New Song," composed by the Henri Capron already mentioned as having performed before Washington in Philadelphia. "Delia" was first published in Philadelphia, in 1793, as part of Moller and Capron's second "Monthly Number." A copy of a later edition, issued by Willig of Philadelphia about 1800, is among the music contained in certain volumes which were once the property of Ann Washington (Mrs. Bushrod Washington) and used by her at Mount Vernon.

The four remaining songs are all of English origin. Even though the United States had gained political independence, it continued for long to be indebted to Europe for musical fame.

The first of these four songs, Samuel Webbe's "The Mansion of Peace," is a gem of the purest water. That it was so great a favorite in America as to have gone through several editions, speaks well for the musical taste of Washington's contemporaries. It figures on at least two programs of which we have a record: a concert at Corre's Hotel, New York, on Jan. 7, 1794, and a concert at Oeller's Hotel, Chestnut Street, Philadelphia, on April 8, 1794.

The last three numbers are excerpts from three ballad-operas which achieved great success in their day. Shield's "Rosina" (first London performance in 1782, first American performance in 1786) and Arnold's "Mountaineers" (first London performance in 1793, first American performance in 1795) were given by wandering troupes in New York, Boston, Providence, Hartford, Philadelphia, Baltimore, New Orleans, and other cities. The "Lullaby" from Storace's "Pirates" (first London performance in 1792, and apparently not given in America as a whole) was a great "drawing-room favorite."

* *

*

Since it is the aim of this collection to satisfy practical and current needs, these have been occasionally permitted to outweigh purely historical considerations. Thus the arranger has taken the liberty of making excisions in both the Sonata by Hewitt and the Rondo by Brown. In the movement from the Reinagle Sonata, on the other hand, he has adhered closely to the composer's autograph—apparently written in haste—making only such non-essential changes and slight corrections as Reinagle himself would presumably have made before letting his work go into print. In all other instances the best available original version has been made the basis of the accompaniment or harmonization.

The variety offered by the pieces contained in even this small collection should suffice for purposes of furnishing incidental music to patriotic pageants and plays,[1] or of providing material for historical programs.[2] No doubt, the times that are mirrored in this music were more heroic and of a vaster import than their musical reflection appears to us today. And yet, we must remember that simple airs and songs of the people have sometimes decided the destinies of nations. The birth of our own nation was thus heralded and accomplished. The music that played its part in that memorable achievement is therefore sure of a lasting place in our hearts.

CARL ENGEL
Chief, Division of Music
Library of Congress

[1] The military and patriotic marches of this collection, including several contained in the Hewitt Sonata, have been published in arrangements for both orchestra and band by G. Schirmer (Inc.), New York.

[2] Additional music and reference material has been published by the U. S. George Washington Bicentennial Commission, and may be obtained through its offices in the Washington Building, Washington, D. C.

TABLE OF CONTENTS

The President's March

Arranged by
James Hewitt (1770-1827)

Philip Phile (d. 1793?)

2

Washington's March

The Toast

(1778)

Francis Hopkinson (1737-1791)

Con spirito

'Tis Wash-ing-ton's health— fill a bump-er a-round, For_ he is our
'Tis Wash-ing-ton's health— loud_ can-nons should roar, And_ trum-pets the
'Tis Wash-ing-ton's health— our_ he-ro to bless, May_ heav-en look

glo-ry and pride; Our_ arms shall in bat-tle with con-quest be crown'd, Whilst
truth should pro-claim; There can-not be found,_ search all the world o'er,_ His
gra-cious-ly down; Oh!_ long may he live_ our hearts to pos-sess,_ And

vir-tue and he's on our side. Our arms shall in bat-tle with con-quest be
e-qual in vir-tue and fame. There can-not be found,_ search all the world
free-dom still call him her own. Oh! long may he live_ our hearts to pos-

crown'd, Whilst vir-tue and he's on our side,_ and he's_ on our side.
o'er,_ His e-qual in vir-tue and fame,_ in vir-tue and fame.
sess,_ And free-dom still call him her own,_ still call_ him her own.

General Burgoyne's March

Tempo di Marcia

Brandywine Quick-Step

Successful Campaign

The Battle of Trenton

"A Favorite Historical Military Sonata Dedicated to General Washington"

(1797)

(abridged)

James Hewitt (1770-1827)

Introduction

Lento

Washington's March (at the Battle of Trenton)

Maestoso

The American Army crossing the Delaware

Ardor of the Americans at Landing

Trumpets sound the Charge

Attack
Presto

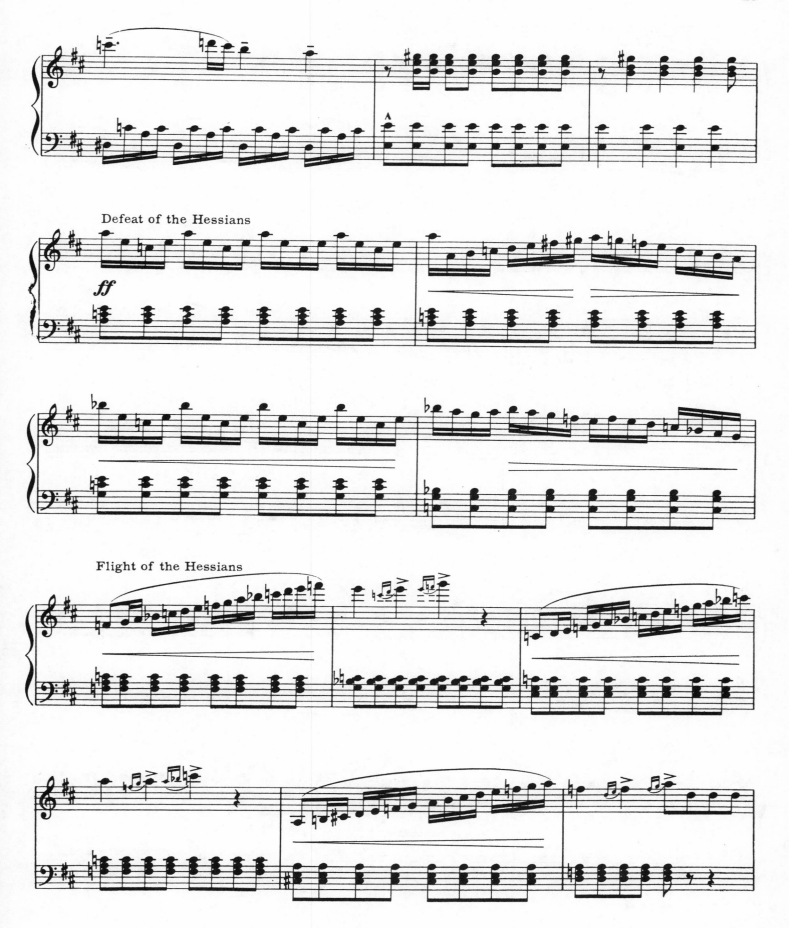

Defeat of the Hessians

Flight of the Hessians

14

The Hessians begging Quarter

The Fight renew'd

16

General Confusion

The Hessians surrender themselves Prisoners of War
Andantino semplice

Roslin Castle

Grief of the Americans for the Loss of their Comrades killed in the Engagement

Lento con espressione

18

Yankee Doodle
Drums and Fifes
Allegro

Quick-Step for the Band

D.C. al 𝄋

Trumpets of Victory

poco riten.

General Rejoicing
Allegro

Sonata

(First movement)

Alexander Reinagle (1756-1809)

Allegro con brio

25

Minuet and Gavotte

Minuet

Tempo di minuetto lento

Alexander Reinagle (1756-1809)

Gavotte

Moderato

Two Minuets

Minuet danced before General Washington

(1792)

Pierre Landrin Duport

Minuet danced before Mrs. Washington

Rondo

(1787)
(abridged)

William Brown

poco marc.

Beneath a Weeping Willow's Shade

(From the "Seven Songs" dedicated to George Washington)

(1788)

Francis Hopkinson (1737-1791)

Be-neath a weep-ing wil-low's shade She sat and sang a-lone,____ Be-

Fond Ech-o to__ her strains re-ply'd, The winds her sor-rows bore,____ Fond

neath a weep - ing wil - low's shade She sat and sang a -
Ech - o to her strains re - ply'd, The winds her sor - rows
lone; Her hand up - on her heart she laid, And
bore; A - dieu dear youth, a - dieu, she cry'd, I
plain - tive was her moan, And plain - tive was her moan.
ne'er shall see thee more, I ne'er shall see thee more.
pp
p
pp
pp
p
pp

The mock-bird sat up-on__ a bough, The

mock-bird sat up-on__ a bough And lis-ten'd to__ her lay,__ Then

to the dis-tant hills he bore__ The dul-cet notes a-way,_____ Then

to the dis - tant hills he bore The dul - cet notes a - way,_____ The

dul - cet notes a - way,_____ The dul - cet notes a - way.

Delia

(1793)

Henri Capron

Soft pleas - ing pains un - known be - fore My beat - ing bos - om__
Some-times at mid - night do I stray Be - neath in - clem - ent__
O tell ye shades that fold my fair And all my bliss con -

feels_____ When I be - hold the bliss - ful bow'r Where dear - est De - lia
skies_____ And there my true de - vo - tion pay To De - lia's sleep-seal'd
tain,_____ Ah why should ye those bless - ings share For which I__ sigh in

dwells,
eyes;
vain,

That
So
But

way I dai-ly__ drive,   I dai-ly drive my__ flock,_____ I
pi-ous pil-grims roam,   So pil-grims night-ly__ roam,_____ So
let me not re-pine,   At fate, at fate re-pine,_____ But

dai -- ly,   I dai -- ly, I dai-ly__ drive my
pil-grims roam,   So pil-grims roam, So pil-grims night-ly
let__ me__ not,   But let__ me__ not At fate, at__ fate re-

flock,
roam,
pine,

48

hap - py vale, Ah hap - py vale, There look and wish, and while I look My
trav - el faint, With trav - el faint, To kiss a - lone the clay - cold tomb Of
griefs im - part, And griefs im - part, She's not your ten - ant, she is mine, Her

cresc.

sighs in - crease the gale.
some lov'd_ fav - 'rite saint.
man - sion_ is my heart.

f

f

When I be - hold the bliss - ful bow'r Where
Some - times at mid - night do I stray Be -
O tell ye shades that fold my fair And

p

dear - est De - lia__ dwells,_____ There look and wish, and
neath in - clem - ent__ skies,_____ And there my true de -
all my bliss con - tain,_____ Ah why should ye those

while I look My sighs in - crease the gale,___ My__
vo - tion pay To De - lia's_ sleep - seal'd eyes,___ To__
bless - ings share For which I__ sigh in vain,___ For_

sighs in - crease the gale.
De - lia's sleep-seal'd eyes.
which I__ sigh in vain.

The Mansion of Peace

(1790?)

Samuel Webbe (1740-1816)

Soft Zeph-yr, on thy bal-my wing

Thy gen-tlest bree-zes hith-er bring,

Her slum-bers

guard   some hand di - vine,   Ah watch her with a care like mine.

Affettuoso

rose, a rose, from her bos-om has stray'd;— I'll
las sil-ly rose,_____ sil-ly rose, hads't thou known___ T'was

p legato

seek to_ re - place it, to re - place it with art; A -
Daph - ne that gave thee, that_ gave thee thy place,

But no, no, no, 'twill her slum - bers in - vade, I'll
Thou ne'er, no ne'er, from thy sta - tion hads't flown; Her

cresc.

wear   it   (fond   youth)___ next   my   heart.
bos - om's   the   man - sion   of

dim.

2. peace.

p

f

Lullaby

(from the Opera "The Pirates")
(1792)

Stephen Storace (1763-1796)

Soave

sempre *p*

Peace-ful

slum-b'ring on the o-cean, Sea-men fear no dan-ger nigh; The winds and
wind tem-pes-tuous blow-ing, Still_ no dan-ger they de-scry; The guile-less

The Bud of the Rose

(from the Opera "Rosina")

(1782)

William Shield (1748-1829)

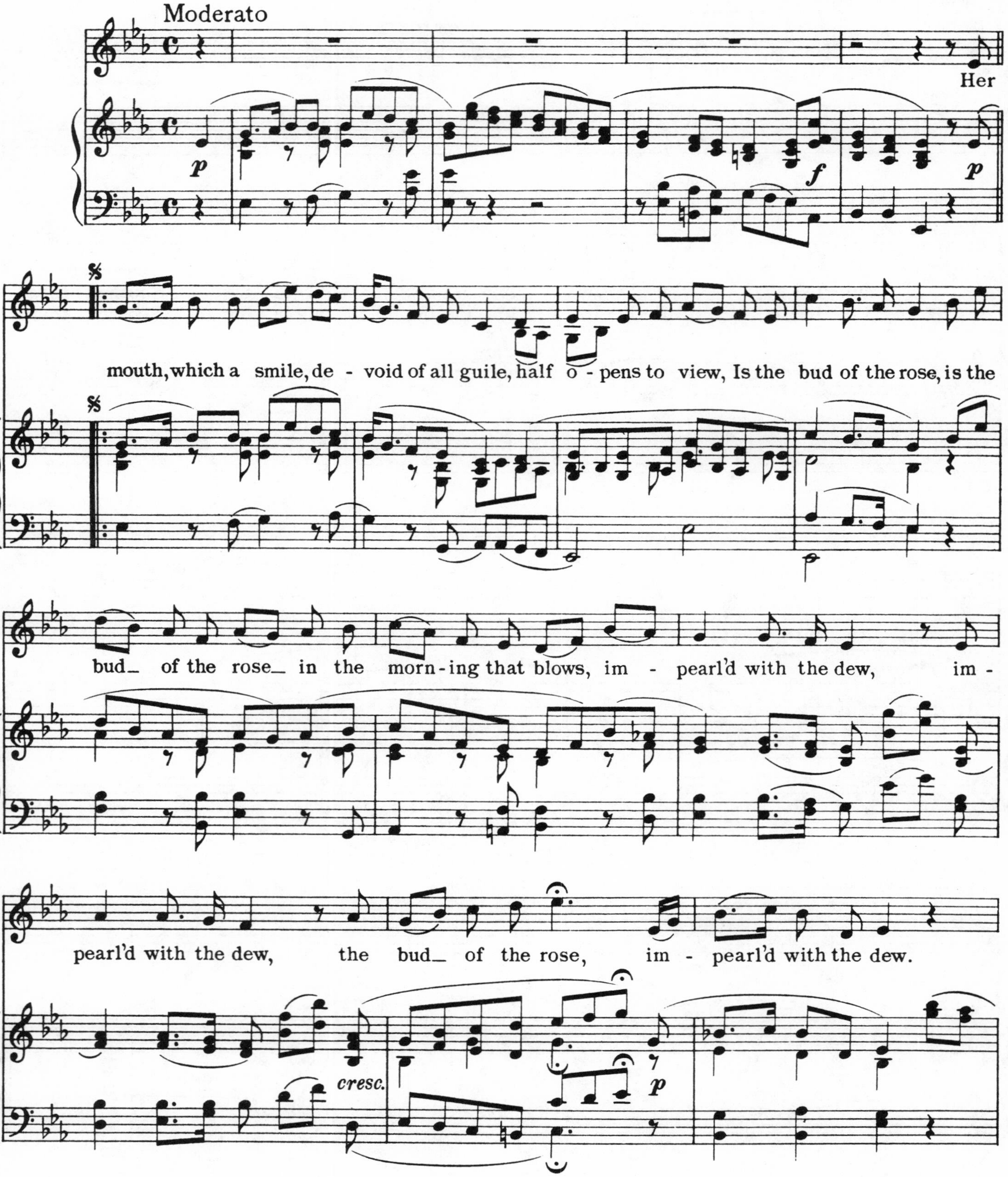
Moderato
Her
mouth, which a smile, de - void of all guile, half o - pens to view, Is the bud of the rose, is the
bud_ of the rose_ in the morn-ing that blows, im - pearl'd with the dew, im -
pearl'd with the dew, the bud_ of the rose, im - pearl'd with the dew.
p
f
p
cresc.
p

Poco più mosso

More fra - grant her breath than the flow'r-scen-ted heath, than the flow'r-scen-ted heath at the

Tempo primo

dawn-ing of day, The haw-thorn in bloom, the lil - y's per-fume,

the lil - y's per-fume, or the blos-soms of May.———————— Her

The Wayworn Traveller

(from the Opera "The Mountaineers")

(1793)

Samuel Arnold (1740-1802)

Faint   and wear - i - ly the way - worn   trav - el - ler___
Tho'   so__ mel - an - chol - y   day has   past__ by,___

plods   un - cheer - i - ly, a - fraid   to   stop,
'twould   be__ fol - ly now to   think   on't   more;

Wan - - d'ring drear - i - ly, a   sad   un - rav - el - ler___
Blithe   and jol - ly, he the   can   holds   fast__ by,___

of   the__ ma - zes tow'rd the   moun - tain's   top;
as   he's__ sit - ting at the   goat - herd's   door;

Doubt - ing,   fear - ing,   while his course he's steer - ing,
Eat - ing,   quaff - ing,   at past la - bours laugh - ing,

Cot - ta - ges ap - pear - ing,   as he's nigh to drop,_____
Bet - ter far by half____ in   spir - its than be - fore,_____

Oh,   how brisk - ly then the way - worn trav - el - ler____
Oh,   how mer - ry then the rest - ed trav - el - ler____

threads   the_ ma - zes tow'rd the moun - tain's   top,
seems   while sit - ting at the goat - herd's   door,

Oh, how brisk-ly then the way-worn trav-el-ler___
Oh, how mer-ry then the rest-ed trav-el-ler___

threads the_ ma-zes tow'rd the moun-tain's top.
seems while sit-ting at the goat-herd's door.

THE STORY OF WASHINGTON

"First in War, First in Peace, First in the Hearts of his Countrymen"

George Washington was truly "First in War," not from any militant disposition of his character, but because of his environment and the times in which he lived.

Born at Bridges Creek, Virginia, February 22, 1732, upon a plantation known later as Wakefield, the boy inherited the blood and stamina of those early colonial pioneers who were almost constantly armed and alert against the invasion of warlike enemies. It was the same blood and stamina that inspired the pioneers of America everywhere to push outward and establish homes amid hostile surroundings.

When George Washington was about three years old, the family moved to what later became Mount Vernon, and when he was seven years old, to a farm on the Rappahannock River, opposite the town of Fredericksburg. It was in this locality that George began his schooling, which consisted principally of reading, writing and arithmetic.

When he was eleven the first great tragedy came into George's life. His father died. Some years later he wanted to go to sea, but his mother persuaded him to give up this idea. Shortly thereafter he went to live with his half-brother Lawrence at Mount Vernon, who had inherited the estate from his father. He soon became deeply interested in surveying and assisted in surveying the lands of Lord Fairfax, who was then living at Belvoir, only a few miles distant. At sixteen he made a month's surveying journey beyond the Blue Ridge mountains.

The military career of Washington began when he was twenty-one. He was commissioned by Governor Dinwiddie to deliver a message to the French on the Ohio, who were encroaching upon what was considered Virginia territory. His subsequent activities during the Braddock campaign are all well known.

At the age of twenty, Washington came into possession of Mount Vernon through the death of his half-brother Lawrence, and the latter's daughter.

In 1759 he married Martha Dandridge Custis and brought her to Mount Vernon which was their home the remainder of their lives, and where he died, December 14, 1799.

George Washington was not only "First in War," but he was among the very first to be prepared for war in the event that England persisted in her crushing attitude toward the colonies.

Washington was one of the leading members of the First Continental Congress.

When called to serve in the Second Continental Congress, he said: "It is my full intention to devote my life and my fortune to this cause."

Upon assuming command of the American Army at Cambridge, July 3, 1775, he solemnly vowed that he would fight until America gained its liberty. This was the beginning of seven years of warfare that was destined to change the history of the world, and bring happiness and prosperity to millions of people.

Never in all history did a commander conduct a war under such discouraging conditions. But discouragements to this hardy pioneer meant nothing. His first work was to convert an aggregation of 16,000 men, mostly farmers, into a disciplined fighting machine.

His next big job was so to arouse the love and patriotism of his soldiers for the cause for which they were fighting, that they might be willing to endure hunger, sickness, disease, and go shoeless and well-nigh naked.

In March, 1776, Washington drove the enemy out of Boston and took a position before New York. When the British thought they had him cornered there, he quietly moved his army of 10,000 across the river. His retreats were as annoying to the enemy as his victories. He could always turn a defeat into a reason for more determined fighting, as shown by the battles of Brandywine and Germantown.

Today all the world applauds his midnight crossing of the ice-flowing Delaware and the dramatic battle of Trenton, where he surprised the Hessians and won a victory that electrified the nation.

From Valley Forge, during the winter of 1777-78, Washington wrote Congress saying of his soldiers: "Their marches might be traced by the blood of their feet." There was never a finer example of the loyalty of soldiers to their leader.

The Battle of Monmouth, in New Jersey, has a remarkable place in history. The fight was almost lost through the disobedience of General Charles Lee. Washington discovered his unsoldierly conduct in time to snatch victory from defeat.

On October 19, 1781, Washington, for all time to come, became a world-figure in military history. That was the day that Cornwallis surrendered at Yorktown. That was the day that America forever won her political and industrial freedom from the oppressing land beyond the sea. It was the true beginning of the United States of America.

And then came peace and quiet. Cannons ceased to roar. Muskets occupied a place of honor behind the kitchen door. Swords were hammered into scythes. Old war horses were hitched to plows and wagons. Crops were planted. Houses and barns were repaired. Churches and schools were put in order.

Washington again became the outstanding American farmer. He was happy at his beloved Mount Vernon, beautifying his estate, enriching his fields, improving his crops and livestock, and doing everything possible to bring happiness and contentment to his loved ones.

The wise and far-seeing statesmanship of Washington was clearly and effectively shown in his last circular letter to the governors of the states, dated June 8, 1783, shortly before resigning his commission. This is a most remarkable document. It contained what he considered the necessary requirements for the very existence of the country.

Always a wise citizen, he kept a watchful eye on the ship of state. It was no great task for this versatile man to change from soldier to statesman. When the time came to place the struggling young country on a more permanent foundation, Washington was made President of the convention which framed the Constitution under which we now live. His advice and diplomacy were invaluable.

And now it was time to elect a President. Washington was unanimously chosen. How he got Congress to function, how he appointed a cabinet, how he created our courts, how he established our entire governmental machinery, and how he won the honor and respect of the entire civilized world has long been a matter of history.

Why was George Washington "First in the Hearts of his Countrymen" and why does he continue to hold that place?

Because he was courageous enough to go to war with one of the most powerful nations on earth for the freedom of his own country. He built an army out of the raw material that came to him from the farms and the towns. He held this army together through almost unbelievable hardships, and with it he outmanœuvered and defeated the generals England sent against him backed by some of the best troops of Europe. By his own example of patient, dogged determination he inspired his men to persevere in the face of privation and discouragement.

Because after independence had been won he gave one of the finest examples of patriotic generosity that the world has ever known. He laid aside his sword and the commission which had placed him at the head of an army and voluntarily returned to the quiet of his beloved home. He sought no honors or personal glory. When he saw his country free he asked nothing from her, but unostentatiously resumed the happy life of a private citizen which had been interrupted by the war.

Because, when the Constitutional Convention was called to frame a new government, he yielded to the importunities of his countrymen and became a delegate to that meeting. He was immediately elected president of the Convention. During those stormy sessions when sectional and other differences divided the delegates so that the existence of the Union was threatened, Washington exerted a powerful influence for compromise that cannot be over-estimated.

Because, as First President of the United States, he started this country on her career as one of the greatest nations in all history. It has been said that the framers of the Constitution created the Presidency of the United States with George Washington in mind as the ideal man for the office.

Because he possessed the qualities of leadership and knowledge of men that inspired confidence among all classes of people. Faith in him was well-nigh universal. Complete understanding existed between him and the people. His general conduct was such as to hold the affection of the public. He was the one man in the country who could harmonize all factions and bring men together in the adjustment of important measures. He quietly and effectively overcame the contentious elements which sought to create national disturbances.

Because, in addition to all this, he was kind, helpful, considerate and generous. In private and public life he was above reproach. He lived and died devoted and faithful to his high ideals of true American manhood.

IN all history no other human being has merited and received such universal homage as George Washington. Nor has any other human being, in the full light of his character and achievements, been so fortunate in escaping criticism and engendering controversy. It is fitting, therefore, that the government of the United States, which he did more than any other man to establish, should promote in 1932, the nation-wide celebration in his honor. This celebration is not intended to add new glories to Washington's name, or place one new leaf in the laurel crown of immortal reverence which his memory inspires. That would be impossible.

The thought behind this Celebration of the Two-Hundredth Anniversary of the Birth of George Washington, is to benefit the living by reviving in the minds and hearts of the American people a just appreciation of the part played by George Washington and his great compatriots in inaugurating a new era of political and social independence that has spread throughout the world.

Responding to this appeal the people of America and other countries have joined with enthusiasm in the plans for celebrating the Bicentennial of Washington's birth. Americans are again learning the lessons of their own history. They are again placing proper values upon the sacrifices and patriotic devotion of the men and women who "brought forth on this continent a new nation, conceived in liberty and dedicated to the proposition that all men are created equal."

By reviving among us the lessons of our national life, by fresh consecration to the fundamentals of the newer freedom of mankind that has shed the glory of equal opportunity upon a world of strife and social and political oppression, by stirring among us all a more exalted appreciation of the priceless heritage left us by the founders of the Republic, the *United States Commission for the Celebration of the Two-Hundredth Anniversary of the Birth of George Washington*, seeks to carry to successful. fulfillment the charge laid upon it by the Congress.

EXITUS ACTA PROBAT

George Washington